SENDING CHRISTMAS CARDS TO HUCK & HAMLET

Sending Christmas Cards to Huck & Hamlet

Poems by

Joseph Mills

Press 53
Winston-Salem

Press 53, LLC
PO Box 30314
Winston-Salem, NC 27130

First Edition

Cover design by Kevin Morgan Watson

Cover art, "Illustration 45," Copyright © 2012 by Alireza Darvish,
used by permission of the artist.

Author photo by Danielle Tarmey

Printed on acid-free paper

ISBN 978-1-935708-53-7

To everyone who has loaned me books
whether you knew it or not.

Acknowledgments

Thanks to the following publications where these poems (or earlier versions) first appeared.

Connotations Press: "At the Veterans Hospital," "The More Deceived," "Shoveling," "Soporific," "Standing Before Shelves of Cookbooks and Trying to Decide What to Make for Dinner"

A Few Lines: "According to My Friend the Astrologer," "At the Transportation Museum of Literature"

Foliate Oak: "the bartender's story," "Charmed," "Lives in Miniature," "Mean," "Salvage," "why some poems make people nervous"

The Innisfree Poetry Journal: "Monsters," "Transmission"

Lowestoft Chronicle: "Jogging Through Jane Austen"

Measure: "Sunday Morning Estate Sale"

The Montucky Review: "What It's Like"

Pembroke Magazine: "Character," "Ode"

Pennsylvania Journal: "The Next Room," "Rodeo," "Strange"

Pirene's Fountain: "Sestina"

Potomac Review: "Ophelia Evaporating," "Posted at Elsinore," "Nature, Indifferent" (as "What Stephen Crane and William Carlos Williams Teach Us About Ophelia")

PrimeNumber Magazine: "Crucible," "Telling Time"

RipRap: "The Last Page of the Dream Journal" (as "Building"), "Three Visions of Richard Brautigan"

Third Wednesday: "Broken (Part I)" (as "Broken"), "Shopping at Frontier Foods," "Sort of Definitive"

And, once again, I'm indebted to the MakeGroup, a wonderful community of artists and friends. And to David Ford of WFDD for including "A Winter Dialogue" in his 2011 TriadArts Holiday Celebration show.

Contents

I. BILDUNGSROMAN

If Librarians Were Honest   3
Lives in Miniature   5
Character   6
Manuals   7
Shopping at Frontier Foods   9
What Westerns Teach You   10
Through This School   11
Broken (Part I)   12
Volatility   13
Standing Before Shelves of Cookbooks and Trying to
    Decide What to Make for Dinner   14
Monsters   16

II. PALIMPSESTS

Mornings in the Castle   19
Transformations   20
Crucible   22
Grumpy   29
The Grace of Dumbo   30
The Lesson of Rumplestiltskin   31
Charmed   32
Beauty, the Beast, and the Blackboard Jungle   33
Telling Time   35
On the Way to Buy Manure for Our Gardens We See
    a "Donkeys for Sale" Sign   36
Shoveling   37
Scaping   38
the bartender's story   39
At the Veterans Hospital   40
The Sea Below   41
A Winter Dialogue   42
What It's Like   43

III. THE COMPANY WE KEEP

Transmission   47
Posted at Elsinore   48
Nature, Indifferent   49
Ophelia Evaporating   50
The More Deceived   51
W.S. Merwin Tells a Story During a Q&A   52
Three Visions of Richard Brautigan   54
Early Morning Riprap   57
The Last Page of the Dream Journal   59
Jogging Through Jane Austen   60
At the Transportation Museum of Literature   61
Fixity   62
Sunday Morning Estate Sale   63

IV. LOOMS

The Next Room   67
Rodeo   68
why some poems make people nervous   69
Mean   70
Strange   72
Soporific   74
When The Poems Came for Dinner   75
Field Trip to the Poetry Discovery Center   76
Sestina   77
Broken (Part II)   78
Sort of Definitive   79
Salvage   80
Ode   81
According to My Friend the Astrologer   82
Sending Christmas Cards to Huck and Hamlet   83

I.

BILDUNGSROMAN

If Librarians Were Honest

... a book indeed sometimes debauched me from my work...
— Benjamin Franklin

If librarians were honest,
they wouldn't smile, or act
welcoming. They would say,
*You need to be careful. Here
be monsters.* They would say,
*These rooms house heathens
and heretics, murderers and
maniacs, the deluded, desperate,
and dissolute.* They would say,
*These books contain knowledge
of death, desire, and decay,
betrayal, blood, and more blood;
each is a Pandora's box, so why
would you want to open one.*
They would post danger
signs warning that contact
might result in mood swings,
severe changes in vision,
and mind-altering effects.

If librarians were honest
they would admit the stacks
can be more seductive and
shocking than porn. After all,
once you've seen a few
breasts, vaginas, and penises,
more is simply more,
a comforting banality,
but the shelves of a library
contain sensational novelties,
a scandalous, permissive mingling
of Malcolm X, Marx, Melville,
Merwin, Millay, Milton, Morrison,
and anyone can check them out,

taking them home or to some corner
where they can be debauched
and impregnated with ideas.

If librarians were honest,
they would say, *No one*
spends time here without being
changed. Maybe you should
go home. While you still can.

Lives in Miniature

On weekend nights, we would beg our parents
to drop us at the mini putt course even though
we hated golf. We wanted to get to the tenth hole,
the one at the back where, if you hit the ball
hard enough, you could punch it over the curb,
through the fence, and into the adjacent field.
Then, you would have to search for it, so
you could look towards the nearby Drive-In,
the one that long ago had stopped showing movies
anyone had heard of to run porn double features.
These were our first glimpses of breasts or what
could be breasts; it was difficult to tell exactly
what the huge moving shapes were, but we knew
they must be something amazing, something
worthy of not just one, but three Xs on the marquee.
We didn't know then how few thrills could match
standing in a field of cow shit on a summer night,
enormous naked women almost within sight,
and bucketfuls of stars spiraling above our heads.

Character

Some characters we never meet for the first time.
We have always known them, just as we heard
about certain family members before we saw them.
At ten, I couldn't have described Uncle Bill who lived
somewhere else—some other town or state or country—
but my parents would talk about him in quiet tones.
Then, one morning, a Cadillac pulled into the drive,
and there he was. Apparently he had decided
the day before, "Sometimes a man needs to see
his goddamn family," and he'd driven all night to do it.
He smoked King Kools, drank Jim Beam, and talked
to my father in a way no one else did. My mother tried
that week to send me to bed early, but I would crouch
on the landing to eavesdrop on the brothers recounting
plots and sub-plots of their lives with voices I recognized
but language I had never heard. Korea had been "cold
as a witch's tit." On one patrol it was "raining
like a cow pissing on a flat rock." Some guy would
"fuck up a two-car funeral." Another was "as useless
as tits on a bull" or "so goddamn stupid he'd fall
into a barrel of boobs and come up sucking his thumb."
Sometimes they became so quiet, I had to move down
the stairs to hear, like when one said something about
having the shakes so bad some mornings he couldn't find
his dick with both hands. Later, in bed, I imagined
driving a Cadillac like a tank through the night,
and, much later, I recognized in books the voices
I had already heard, characters who had stories
they needed to tell so badly they would seek out
someone they knew would sit in the dark and listen.

Manuals

We snuck Harold Robbins,
Erica Jong, and Danielle Steele
from our parents' bedrooms
into ours and burrowed
underneath the covers
to study certain scenes.
In school, our teachers insisted
Shakespeare, Twain, and Hardy
offered valuable life lessons,
and maybe they did,
but we weren't learning
anything specific from them.
Where did you put your hand?
What happened after the kiss?
We snickered in class,
as we knew was expected,
when Iago suggested Desdemona
had been busy somewhere
"making the beast with two backs,"
and we knew in theory,
thanks to family life class,
how the beast was made.
Yet, we also understood
we were missing a great deal
of information. So we turned
to the few books in the house,
gleaning what we could
from passages where someone
throbbed triumphantly
or felt herself dissolving
into her hot liquid center.
It still wasn't always clear
what alchemy made a body do
what these bodies were doing,

but we knew these books
must have something to offer.
After all, they were the ones
our parents kept near,
and when we picked them up,
they instantly spread open
to certain pages, as if ready
and wanting to be read.

Shopping at Frontier Foods

As a kid, when I became impatient
at the grocery check-out, my mother
would say, *You should pity the cashier;*
after all, she's always at the end of the line.

No. That never happened. I read that
in one of the mildewed *Reader's Digests*
we kept above the toilet. They featured
clever funny families, not ones like ours

where the mother spat loudly how
she always picked the slowest line,
the one filled with idiots and people
trying to cut in front or rip you off.

My mother's life stood a loaded gun
in a world with enemies in every aisle
which is probably why I liked *Kung Fu*
and paperback Westerns. Those men—

the monk, Indians, and old scouts—
saw the big picture. They never lost it
even during an ambush. They just did
what had to be done. They were the ones

I wanted to shop with because I knew
they would calmly accept people
in the express lane with too many items
or calmly step up and shoot them dead.

What Westerns Teach You

Always sit with your back to the wall.
Pay attention to the weather and birds.
If you're too wounded to walk, you can crawl.
The worst job is behind the herd.

Pay attention to the weather and birds.
Someone knows you in every town.
The worst job is behind the herd.
You can never avoid a showdown.

Someone knows you in every town.
The land can be read like a book.
You can never avoid a showdown.
Some wounds are as bad as they look.

The land can be read like a book.
The heart has little to do with the face.
Some wounds are as bad as they look.
The world's a violent and beautiful place.

The heart has little to do with the face.
If you're too wounded to walk, you can crawl.
The world's a beautiful and violent place.
Always sit with your back to the wall.

Through This School

Every August, the principal gives
the same speech to the families
stacked on the gym bleachers.
Through this school comes our future,
senators, mayors, doctors, and lawyers.
He doesn't mention through the school
also comes future plumbers, nurses,
and custodians, and there's not a word
about the future thieves, deadbeats,
and arsonists, or that some of the ones
who go through do so with difficulty,
blocking the way like kidney stones
until they're painfully passed. No one
points out a manager at McDonald's
or DMV clerk could say the same.
We go through the doors and halls
together then tell ourselves that we—
we take the roads less travelled by.
But that speech comes later. In June.
In August, the parents sit, listening
and fantasizing one day their kids
will be mentioned as famous alumni
while, next to them, the children
wait, with varying degrees of patience,
knowing this isn't really about them,
but eager to pass through towards
the unspeakable future that will be.

Broken (Part I)

She talked about broken grammar
as if the sentences had been working
fine until we got our hands on them.
No wonder she was annoyed with us.
We weren't students, but vandals,
joywriting into telephone poles,
or, at best, klutzes, dropping pieces
on the floor or cracking them
against door jambs and tabletops.

Or maybe she thought of us as animals
loose in the china shop of language,
smashing fragile syntax,
chewing and drooling on parts of speech
that were hundreds of years old,
treating dumbly
the grammar we didn't appreciate
and certainly couldn't be trusted with,
not until we had been properly broken.

Volatility

Finally in Chemistry lab, we began
to learn more interesting things
than the facts in calcified textbooks,
especially when the teacher left
to have a smoke or make a call
and we could experiment with how
acetate could be spread across
those black counters and ignited
to create a sudden block of fire,
or methane gas could be sucked
from Bunsen burner hoses
into plastic syringes to make
miniature flamethrowers.
For a change, we paid attention
to the concepts on the board:
*flashpoints, melting points,
combustion, incineration.*
We understood these
would be good to know
since already some of us
had begun to burn, and,
if the priests and poets
were to be believed,
eventually we all would.

Standing Before Shelves of Cookbooks and Trying to Decide What to Make for Dinner

Most of these I've never used,
although each time I bought one
I was convinced that I would,
just as I thought I would read
the pile of parenting books
that now spills under the bed,
or the texts on physics,
stars, and string theory
stacked next to my desk.
I used to check out hundreds
of library books, hoping somewhere
in the pages would be the advice
I needed to make something
with the ingredients of my life,
yet each day ends up being
another hasty improvisation
with nothing measured cleanly
and no clear sequence to the steps.
Still, I continue to believe
in the idea of simple solutions,
ones as elegant as a wheel.
I remember how someone said
the best Italian dishes have no more
than four ingredients with the key
being freshness and quality,
how Archimedes claimed he could
move the world with a long enough lever
and a solid place to stand,
how the most powerful sentence
in the Bible is "Jesus wept."
So later, after dinner, whatever it is,
I will navigate the dark bedrooms
of my children, threading past
piles of books, toys, and clothes,

until I stand before them,
the daughter and the son,
each asleep, wrapped in sheets
like loaves of fresh bread,
and I will murmur a kind of prayer:
May you recognize the wheel
of your days. May your faith
and friendships be flavored
with tears May you find love
like a lever and a place to stand
together. May you have a life as
satisfying as a good Italian dish.

Monsters

As I leave, my son yells, "Daddy, watch out
for other cars and monsters." It's good advice.
I tell him I will, and I'll pay special attention
to monsters in cars. I've seen quite a few:
tailgaters, speeders, drunks, teenagers
weaving and mooning, an old woman
whacking a middle finger against a window,
saliva strands whipping from her mouth.
And there were those nights years ago
when we couldn't go to anyone's house,
so we would park next to the woods,
then snuffle and grapple each other's pelts,
aware of the dangers, scared, but unable
to resist our beautiful monstrous selves.

II.

PALIMPSESTS

Mornings in the Castle

The morning is going the way
it does, lately. I am urging
the kids to eat breakfast, looking
for shoes, and collecting papers.
They are getting up yet again
to ask for something, ignoring
my pleas to finish their cereal,
asking for some other thing,
and suddenly someone is yelling.

I'm always surprised by the rage,
how quickly it rises as if freed
from the depths like a Balrog
unleashed by love's mining.
My children aren't. They know,
having learned from books
TV, and films, monsters are
everywhere, in the darkness,
in the woods, and in the people
you love and you know love you.
This is the story's unexpected turn,
not how we become monstrous,
snarling, snapping, and spewing,
but how we become mirrors,
reflecting one another's ugliness
in ways that we can barely face.

Transformations

I used to pity Rapunzel, unjustly imprisoned,
a victim and symbol of a repressive society
that locks women away until they must use
the emblems of femininity to try to escape,

and then we had children, ones who didn't act
like the parenting books suggested they would,
who seemed instead to have come from the dark
fairy-tales, those of the Grimms, not Disney.

With little warning, they would transform
into various were-beasts, bears, wolfs, dogs,
or fierce-beaked birds. They barked and bit,
howled and hurled whatever came to hand.
They were immune to reason, admonitions,
pleas, sarcasm, laughter, feigned equanimity.
Spanking only annoyed them and made them
more ferocious, no hug could last long enough
to calm them, and we couldn't find the spell
or incantation that would charm them quiet.

When they refused to remain in time-out
and instead stalked us through the house,
snarling, scratching, hitting, and kicking,
we locked them away, high in their bedrooms,
where they clawed and hammered at the walls.
Eventually, they would change back to the form
of children and call out for help, telling passersby
they had been cruelly imprisoned, their voices
and faces so sweet even we sometimes believed it.

Each story transforms the ones that came before,
so now I wonder what Rapunzel might be
capable of, and what the castle looks like inside.
Are the tower stairs covered with combs, scissors,
clothing, ripped paper, whatever she could throw
before someone managed to get the door closed?
Does the laundry room have a hamper of towels,
used to wipe the places where she has spat?
And, in the kitchen, is the trash full of wine bottles,
ones shared by Rapunzel's parents late at night,
as they talk about what to do, allowing themselves
to let their hair down and say horrible things,
things they must keep behind locked doors?

Crucible

i.

Tell us a story, the children plead,
as they burrow under their covers,
and the parents, although they know
it's a delaying tactic, always agree.
Listen, they say, once upon a time
there were girls and boys like you,
scared and resourceful, disobedient
and loved, and there were parents,
like us, trying to keep them safe
and warm and fed, but they failed,
so the children had to leave to fight
monsters and giants, witches and wolves,
and when they came back home
sometimes they found their parents
had died, but not you, you never will.

ii.

Yes, there is evil
in the world, some
directed at you
and you can do
nothing to avoid it.
Beware of strangers.
Don't judge by appearances.
None of these will help.
Evil will do what evil does,
striking you down
even when you don't
bite into the apple,
and if you're lucky,
you survive, sometimes
unconscious, sometimes
in a tower (after all
there are so many ways
to be locked up),
but still alive, if not
warm, at least waiting.

iii.

You prefer beauty
to the point of wanting
someone comatose
instead of the village girl
who dances according
to her own desires

because you believe
you will be the one
to wake her, the one
to make her move,
your vivifying kiss,
your animating presence.

This is the mirror
of the tale. Stop
looking at her,
imagining the feel
of that skin, and listen.

iv.

Forget they're animals.
Forget the easy jokes
about property crimes.
Ignore slogans like:
"Avoid extremes" or
"Find the middle way."
Consider only the bare
element. A woman,
a blonde stranger,
eats and sits and sleeps
in the bed where you've shared
your most intimate moments.
Call her intruder
or mistress.
Call her daughter-in-law
or doubt.
Call her longing
or desire.
Whatever she's called,
she will come,
and afterwards
nowhere will be
just right again.

v.

When you get home
after stealing and killing
to feed your family,
you'll take an ax
to memory,
hacking down
the evidence
and burning
the green stalks;
the smoke will be
seen for miles
ensuring an audience
for you to recount
what happened,
and what happened
will become the tale
you tell.

vi.

Ignore the housing materials;
pay attention to the statistics.
Whatever gets built
brute force knocks down
two out of three times.

This is enough
to keep yourself fed
and something to remember
when you lock the door
before going to bed.

vii.

Blood, puberty,
sex, violence,
sometimes it may be
about these,
but always
the family dies.
No matter what
we do or have
in the basket,
no matter who
happens to pass by
at the last minute.
Blame the wolves
among us, famine,
viruses, poor vision,
or tell the story
so the mother
of your mother
survives this
particular ending
but we all know
where each path ends.
Burn everything
away; this remains
the bone of the story
on which we choke.

Grumpy

What the hell are we to do with a casket of crystal and gold?
It was custom-made, so the funeral place that sold
it won't take it back. It's small of me, I know,
to seem concerned with money afterwards. I'm supposed
to be glad she's alive, found her prince
and all that muck, but I find it hard since
we've been stuck with the bill. We leave our jobs, get this thing made,
pledge an eternal vigil at the grave,
then she gets kissed, jumps up, and buggers off.
A wave. That's what we get from her and her toff.
We could dump something in it—fish, dirty laundry—
or see what we could get on eBay,
but for now it sits under the trees collecting dust.
Occasionally we see one another through the glass,
faces distorted by emptiness and grief.
We're all bashful now if bashful means ashamed at having believed
we could be more than what we are—comic relief,
sideshow freaks,
a useful source of shelter, a bed, food,
but always just a temporary stay in the woods.

The Grace of Dumbo

The fat and stupid
can fly.

It just takes faith,
if only in a feather,
belief by a mind
annealed by grief
or a night's drinking.

And not even that.
It takes
nothing.

This may be
a comfort
but also
a warning.

Grace comes
unforeseen,
unforeseeable.

Good works
pious words
fairness of face
mean nothing.

The fat and stupid
inexplicably ascend.

The Lesson of Rumplestiltskin

He wasn't naïve. He knew
beauty rarely pays
its debts, but the title
misled him. Cinderella,
Snow White, Goldilocks,
Little Red Riding Hood.
When you get top billing,
the story is yours.
So he thought he could
force a hard trade,
blood for gold,
but he couldn't resist
stringing her along,
and he couldn't keep
his mouth shut.
Whisper into your hands,
a wall, a tree;
someone will hear.
Someone is always
listening. Someone
knows your name.

Charmed

Uninterested in women, he couldn't be bothered
to dance with those gathered by his father.
Instead, he stayed on the margin, pretending
to be aloof, posing in one of the uniforms he loved.
But, when she arrived, late, as tentative as a calf,
most importantly, alone, he knew at first sight
here was someone who understood what it meant
to dissemble, to wear borrowed clothing, to hide
one's longing. He recognized what they could be
for one another was useful, and this is why
he agreed to marry. We know what happened
afterwards. Supposedly. But the lack of details
is suspicious. Why do we never hear about kids?
Why does everyone still call her Cinderella?
What happened to his mother, the godmother,
the step-sisters' father? We know instinctively
not to concern ourselves with these, and this
may be the animal truth underneath the glitter:
a story, relationship, happiness itself, lasts
if we're careful not to ask the right questions.

Beauty, the Beast, and the Blackboard Jungle

The teacher explains the book
retells Beauty and the Beast,
a common exercise from *Jane Eyre*
to *As Good as It Gets*. Someone
worthwhile has been buried under
the brute, the jerk, the old man,
and love will redeem and reveal him.
Of course this story comforts women,
offering them reassuring fantasies
about transformations they can trigger.
As for men, they know how cruel
their actions look and how they hurt
others, and yet they continue to do it,
so the story offers the justification
they cannot help themselves, and
the solace they will be rewarded
anyway. And, obviously, both
are equally imprisoned, and must
free one another. So, this, of course,
reaffirms marriage making it
liberation rather than bondage.

The teacher pauses to allow time
for everyone to fully appreciate
these comely insights. A few
take notes, then someone growls,
"What a bunch of bullshit."
Before anyone can respond,
the voice repeats, "Bull. Shit."
It comes from a student in back
who has never spoken and usually
appears to be indifferent or asleep.
"It's not just the asshole, but Barbie

who needs to hook up soon.
Like my grandma used to say,
The clock starts at first blood;
a bloom gone is gone for good."
Most snicker or act indignant,
but one person seems contemplative,
as if, for the first time, looking
closely at something familiar and
realizing it is not what it appears.

Telling Time

A tale, like a rock,
over the years,
becomes smooth
from constant rubbing;
edges and corners abrade
until it seems no more
than a glossy ornament,
but hold it to your ear,
you can still hear
the ticking within.

Whatever gets polished
away—the violence
we do to one another
and ourselves, the cutting
off of toes to try to fit
into a slipper, the dancing
to death in red hot shoes,
the pulling out of tongues—
this remains: the clock
will strike midnight,
the crocodile is near,
the last petal is falling.
Hurry, each story says,
you don't have much time.

On the Way to Buy Manure for Our Gardens We See a "Donkeys for Sale" Sign

Betsy says Bob wants a donkey
and she wants chickens and I

think I'm supposed to name
an animal because that's how

fairy tales go and by the end
our menagerie will work together

to overcome some fierce beast
terrorizing the neighborhood,

but I don't have the time to give
my dog the attention she deserves,

so I don't want another animal,
especially one that might unleash

mythical problems, although imagining
Bob balanced atop a donkey,

his long legs kneeing around his chin
or scoring the ground, and Betsy's chickens

getting loose to lay eggs, ones we need
to find before they hatch all kinds

of trouble, I recognize that story
might be wondrous to live as well.

Shoveling

A man in the shape of my father sits
in my peripheral vision, drinking beer
and watching me shift around the truck bed
trying to figure out how best to shovel a load
of manure into the yard. I can hear him
muttering, *I thought I sent you to college
so you wouldn't have to do stuff like this.*
When I insist that it's more rewarding
than grading papers, he shakes his head,
*If I had known this is what you would do
with your life, I could have shown you how
in an afternoon and bought myself a boat.*
I resist saying he did a pretty good job
demonstrating how to fling crap around
when we were young; it would be a dig
he would laugh at then mull over later
until it enraged him. We can't ever seem
to let some things stay buried. Instead
I suggest, *It's nice to have it be a choice.*
He shrugs, *Say what you want. Shit is shit.*

Scaping

He stands in the back of the flatbed,
holds up a plant in each hand, and asks,
"What are these called?" He repeats
the question, speaking more slowly
in case the accent is interfering again.
Finally the foreman looks over and says
with equal deliberation, "I'll tell you
what those are called. Those are called
get to fucking work. You don't need
to know what those are fucking called.
You just need to put them in the ground."

The rest of the crew stands and listens,
shovels in hands to show they're working
or ready for something, a fight or hole to fill.
The foreman turns back to his phone;
the man drops the plants off the truck.
Now he knows. Those are called things
that need to be put into the ground.
Those are called things he doesn't need
to know. Those are called why he's here.
In any language, it's the same: To be
transplanted means having to endure
hands pruning things away. Even
names. Even the desire to know names.

the bartender's story

sure everyone has got a story
and most of them are boring
they had a job they didnt like
or one they did but something
went wrong then more somethings
one sadass litany after another
of how their lives didnt turn out
like they thought they would

ask a kid what they want to be
and see how many say bartender
but i dont even remember now
what i would have said there were
kisses kids bills then the years change
and the days dont thats my story
or maybe i heard it from someone
in here its hard to know anymore

At the Veterans Hospital

She says she wonders what has happened to The Book of
Life and The Book of the Dead now that everything's gone
digital. It's hard to imagine God swiping a Kindle, or St. Peter,
that maître-d' at the Gates, looking up arrivals on his iPad. But
why, he asks, do these seem any stranger than vellum, or
parchment, or paper? We have always been told this world is
virtual, a simulation of another. At this she starts to cry, and
when he places a hand on her new leg, she pushes it off,
saying, *This is not real.* Her tone is hard to read, and he doesn't
know if she means the limb, the crying, the empathy, the
room, the world. *Maybe not,* he says, *but it's what we have.*

The Sea Below

The story's skin changes
chameleon-like
so it can appear to be
a parable of art
or invention, ambition
or awakening,
but the bones
of its skeleton
stay fixed:

how even in times of danger,
we get distracted by joy
and forget where we are,
chasing the ball
into the road,
playing with the gun
found in the closet,
or dancing on a roof,
the landscape below
unrolled like butcher paper,

how our gifts
destroy,

how we fly together,
such a brief time
until the inevitable turn
when one of us falls
and one must watch,

how always there is
the sea below.

A Winter Dialogue

We decide to take a break from the eating, drinking,
and arguing—our traditional holiday pastimes—
to walk around the ice-encased neighborhood.
In the hallway, we sort through the piles of coats,
hats, and gloves, pulling out what we think we need,
and when I get to the door my father calls me back
to drape a scarf around my neck. In my forties,
I don't like scarves anymore than when I was six,
but, now, having kids, I recognize what his fingers
are trying to say as they adjust the wool, and, I hope,
he recognizes what I'm trying to say by not moving.
It's not much, but since neither of us needs anything
the other can buy, we try to exchange what we can,
a protective touch and a willingness to be touched.

What It's Like

I had thought it must be like
having random pages torn out,
so it becomes difficult to remember
character names, plots, and settings,
until one night, washing dishes together,
her muscle memory smoothly
moving her from sink to cupboard,
she stopped in the middle of drying
the large stainless steel colander
she had bought years before,
and said, "You know how sometimes,
at a party, you'll be in the kitchen
talking to someone for a long time
and when you go back out
everyone has left without you
knowing it. You had thought
they were still there, and the party
was still going, and then
when you go into the living room,
you suddenly feel as if . . . as if . . ."
She stood and turned the colander
in her hands then, after a moment,
she put it back in the sink as if deciding
that probably was a safe choice
for something like that, whatever it was.

III.

The Company We Keep

Transmission

We ignore the emails from the Nigerian banker,
the manager for the British National Lottery,
the Chinese immigrant offering millions to help
launder his fortune, but we'll click on the link
from our spouse or sibling. It's those we love
who infect us, as anyone with children knows.
Hamlet could have walked away from Elsinore,
if it hadn't been his father, his mother, his uncle,
and they insisted on keeping him close enough
to bring everyone down. Guard the battlements
and put in firewalls, install alarms and cameras,
stockpile weapons; these will help you feel
as if you're doing something, but what will come
will come from family and friends. Love pulls
us into blood; love is how we all are breeched.

Posted at Elsinore

Gertrude comes in and breaks the news
about how the girl was picking cowslips,
bluebells, marigolds, and these details
make it clear that people were watching.
She is repeating a report, but no one asks
why the reporter didn't pull Ophelia out.
Perhaps they have come to expect this
from the paparazzi staking out the castle,
who feel their job is to record the events
rather than become involved, or they know
the writers wouldn't ruin a good story
with direct action. "Girl Falls In Stream"
doesn't sell many magazines. But maybe
some didn't even notice, too busy writing
the names of flowers to add as local color,
anxious to get something filed before
the cock crowed, too absorbed in words
to see her face slip underneath the surface.

Nature, Indifferent

In painting after painting,
we see her with flowers,
walking through meadows,
the nature girl, unhinged
by Elsinore's unnatural doings,
but what if it happened
in reverse? As the poet says,
we cannot go to the country
for the country will bring us
no peace. With Polonius dead,
killed by Hamlet, now exiled,
what does nature do? Bloom
and grow, oblivious, as always,
to our sorrows, injustices,
and outrageous fortunes.
Perhaps it isn't the evil
that men do, but the lark,
the nightingale, the flowering
dogwood's iridescent petals
with their indifferent beauty,
that drives a person mad.

Ophelia Evaporating

They may have gotten it wrong,
all those reports of Ophelia
suggesting she drowned herself
because of her disappointments,
the death of her father, the madness
of her lover. It may have been
an accident as she stepped into
the stream deliberately, thinking
a little water therapy might help
clear her head and ease the tensions
collected in her shoulders and neck.
She might have only meant to stay
a few minutes before climbing out
to make her way back to Elsinore
where she would stamp footprints
across the castle's gray flagstones,
a trail of small wet hearts leading
to her room then evaporating away.

The More Deceived

At the baby shower, her mother passed around a photo of when she had sung and played lead guitar in The More Deceived. Someone said, *Say goodbye to ever fitting into leather pants like that again.* The picture had been taken the last night of the town's summer festival, the one that was cancelled a few years later, and it had been the only time, they had performed "Larkin Was Right" to people who had seen her grow up, ones who had smiled at her as she sat in timeout on the curb outside of the Big Boy and who had pretended not to be checking her out after she got breasts. She had screamed the lines, *They fuck you up, your mom and dad. They may not mean to but they do*, and, for once, the sound system had been clear. She imagined they could hear her twenty miles away in Greenville. She sang better than she ever had or would again since the band broke up a month later when Katie decided to go to college after all. When she had finished that song, holding the last note as long as she could, then standing defiantly at the stage's edge, ready for the scorn and hatred, they had applauded, some even prying themselves out of their blue folding chairs to stand, and she had been appalled. Now, someone was asking if she meant to name the baby Ophelia, and her mother was smiling, but she found herself unable to answer, disconcerted by a growing realization of just how much someone can be deceived.

W.S. Merwin Tells a Story During a Q&A

Some question reminds him of the last time
he went to France, how he ate with a man
who told him about digging in his land
exploring a limestone chimney before
the winter arrived and how frost and wind
made this kind of work difficult to bear.

Keeping the hole small, as if to bury
a pet, the man uncovered glass, centimes,
potshards, shells, arrowheads, and this, Merwin
said, wasn't surprising. Almost every man
understood others had lived there before.
No one ever used the term "virgin land."

You lived on it and one day passed the land
on to the children that your wife would bear.
He had thought this was how it was before
he began digging, but the earth sometimes
has a different story to tell a man.
It keeps mysteries from water and wind

that, once uncovered, provide a window
to some oblique drama staged on the land.
Like the bones of a Neanderthal man
he found arranged next to those of a bear.
They had been interred there at the same time,
but why? What ritual had this been for?

And, there was something more puzzling. The four
femurs had been switched. At this point Merwin
stopped to give the audience enough time
to imagine that distant age and land
where at a grave site the legs of a bear
had been exchanged for the legs of a man.

After he found the skeletons, the man
tried to cover them again, but, before
long, scientists came and stripped the site bare,
boxing the embracing animal twins
and hauling the bones away in a Land
Rover. An old story in modern times.

A man raised his hand asking when this was
and for more details. It seemed outlandish.
The tale's bearer grinned and said that was time.

Three Visions of Richard Brautigan

i.

Driving along a back road
I notice the tall thin figure
standing next to a duffel,
and, although I promised
my wife I would never
pick up hitchhikers,
I figure dead ones
don't count,
so I stop.

He sits in the passenger seat,
his hands folded
like large origami birds,
and I wait for him to speak
about fame and fishing,
his life and death,
about what is
in the bag
and where we need
to go,
but he just looks out
the side window
as if we're driving along
a road he's never seen
or one he's been on
many times.

ii.

During a Christmas party
the DJ plays some BeeGees,
and everyone at my table
yells and struts
to the dance floor.
Afterwards, I notice,
along the back wall,
the tall man in the cowboy hat,
and I realize
he too knows this music.
Michael Jackson and Madonna
were at the top of the charts
the year he killed himself,
and long after the Summer of Love,
there were all those nights
sitting alone in Japanese bars,
drawing fish on cocktail napkins,
and listening to yet another
Hall and Oates song.

iii.

He holds out his hands
as if they're cuffed together
and scraps of paper
flow from his palms
like a magic trick.
Please, he says,
without moving his lips,
Take some,
before they disappear.

Early Morning Riprap

In my dream
Gary Snyder is dead.
              I don't know how
                    and I don't know how
                          I know and I don't know
                          how I ended up
          in Japan
          a river of mourners
          reciting his work
                          although I don't know how
                          I know what they're saying

Afterwards
I stay in bed
              trying to remember
              poems I used to know.

                          I still have some titles
                          a few phrases

          I went into the Maverick Bar

                          And dammmit, that's just what
                          I've gone and done

                    stay together
                    learn the flowers
                    go light

but nothing whole.

          I think about calling Sean
          ask if he remembers
          that time at Snyder's place

the former Shinto temple
moved to the woods
above Nevada City

       the weekend we spent
       drinking beer
       eating brownies
       talking about Jersey suburbs
       bear scat
       Lew Welch's suicide

     but I wonder if I should check
     the news first or call around

find out if anyone is dead
and how it happened.

The Last Page of the Dream Journal

When I reach the last page of my dream journal,
I wonder what to do with it, so I ask three friends,
and the first one says, "Tell them to a therapist,"
and the second says, "Make one into a movie,"
and the third says, "Start at the beginning again
and write over the top of the old ones," and this
makes the first two friends say, "Yeah, do that,"
and maybe I should end this poem by saying,
"And I dreamt that I did" or "then I woke up,"
but instead I sit on a bench and remember once,
in an airport, how I overheard a father quizzing
his son about the ceiling's design and if its rods
were concave or convex. It made me jealous.
Why hadn't I studied engineering or been smarter
about how I travelled and talked with my children?
If I understood something about architecture,
maybe I would be more efficient in connecting
the ceiling of dreams to the walls of friends
to the floors of poems. Instead I try to join
the pieces by trial and error, but I never know
how snug I can tighten them or the weight
each can hold until something shears away.

Jogging Through Jane Austen

He has run through most of the books
in the libraries around town and discovered
the best places tend to be in British novels
of the nineteenth century if they aren't
set in London or the industrial north.
Twentieth century literature is too riven
with wars, class struggles, grammatical
experiments, and identity upheavals.
The ground shifts so much that it's easy
to turn an ankle. He tried working out
in the Renaissance for a while, attracted
by the access to Shakespeare everywhere
but found the climates unpredictable.
Weather and governments would shift
so abruptly it was difficult to get home.
Plus people wouldn't leave him alone.
In a world of witches, no one is strange,
even a man in Nikes and black nylon shorts.
So now he sticks mostly to Austen novels,
loping along paths between Bath and Bristol.
If anyone notices, they're either too polite
or too skeptical to say anything. Or maybe,
in this milieu, no one can admit they've seen
a bare-legged man covered with sweat,
scissoring purposefully across the countryside.
In these stories, he feels safe. He knows
where they go, the twists and turns, everything
as comfortable as broken-in running shoes.

At the Transportation Museum of Literature

We broke in, intending to just look around,
but, as the poet says, beer leads on to beer,
so, after trying to hotwire a cheap replica
of a car driven by Paradise and Moriarty,
we declaimed Shakespeare on the raft
salvaged from a Louisiana scrapyard,
then tagged our names across a carriage
from some Austen novel and the ass
of the Trojan horse, and, in the morning,
after waking in the coffin from the Pequod,
we crawled back outside and soon discovered
we were embarrassed now to have to walk,
like Joads, we, who had held the Argo's wheel
and opened the throttle of the Wabash Cannonball.

Fixity

When we reread a book, the characters act
the way they did before, the same choices,
the same results. Romeo still kills himself
too soon, and Roxanne still realizes too late.
No wonder we want to yell at some of them
for making the same dumb ass decisions
over and over. After a while, we're bored,
then contemptuous of these lives looping
like trains on a set schedule, and maybe
this is how God feels watching us run
along our story-lines. But no matter how
often we open the book, when Romeo sees
Juliet or Ishmael sees the whale, for them,
it is always the first time, always exciting,
always fresh. So, maybe we should feel,
not frustration or even pity, but envy
of their blissful ignorance. They live
their lives anew each page, feeling a sense
of possibility, while we are stuck, fixed,
wriggling on the pin of what we know.

Sunday Morning Estate Sale

Browsing the piles scattered on the ground—
thrillers, cookbooks, old *Newsweeks* and *Times*—
I find a paperback Western for a dime
and throw it on a dish my wife has found.

The weathered cowboy, who just then had been
leaving the saloon, staggers and falls down.
He curses when he sees his horse is gone
as is the stable and hotel. Again.

The few remaining buildings sit askew.
These earthquakes seem to happen more and more.
The preacher talks of end times, and the whore
says that may be, but there's still work to do.

The cowboy watches warriors walk past,
then workers from the railroad wander by;
some talk of starting fresh, and some will try
to find where in the story they were last.

He considers returning for more gin,
sitting in the dark with the old-timers;
instead he gets a shovel from a miner
in case his horse needs digging out again.

He joins the crowd in the disheveled street
all trying to keep their footing in a world
that bucks and shifts as if some casual God
had gotten bored and tossed it on a heap.

With what's left, they'll try to rebuild the town.
It's all they can or know to do these days.
My wife holds up the book before she pays.
I shake my head. She drops it on the ground.

IV.

Looms

The Next Room

Through the wall comes laughter,
applause, even an occasional whoop,
and you know your students feel
they have registered for the wrong class.
Maybe if they had put 202 instead of 201,
they'd be there, on the other side,
laughing, crying, meeting their future
spouses, having wondrous epiphanies,
and discovering unfamiliar subjects
that will become their life's work.
Instead, they're stuck here, turning back
to chapter six to review material
they should have learned weeks ago,
material they suspect the next room
has woven into award-winning songs
they play on lutes and drum machines,
ones that go viral on the internet and
touch the hearts of criminals, the poor,
the suicidal, the dissatisfied in rooms
all around the world, including this one.

Rodeo

A student smacks the book on to his desk,
looks around, and says, "I hate poetry."
Several nod, thrilled to have someone voice
what they feel. It's not yet a mob, but if
Poetry were coaxed into an alley
I bet some of them would follow to help
beat the hell out of it. So, I ask, "Why?
What has it ever done to you? Come on
to your sister? Welch on a loan? Promise
it could help you lose weight or get a job?"
Most start to laugh, not recognizing, I,
like a rodeo clown, have drawn away
the mad bull's attention, so Poetry
can scramble between the rails to safety.

why some poems make people nervous

the ones
with short lines
move so quickly
down the page
not even
punctuation
to slow them
they seem
out of control
dangerous
suicidal
plunging
towards the end
taking
the reader
with them

Mean

For almost an hour they've argued
about what the poem means,
and, although they've reached
a consensus, treating interpretation
as a kind of democratic exercise
or statistical problem, now
at the end of class, they turn to me
for the answer. They're sure I know.
If I say I don't, they won't believe me.
And they shouldn't. I do know
what the poem means to me today,
but I also know that it used to mean
something different several years ago
when I first read it. Some poems are fish
finning away when you try to grab them,
but, if you can hook, net, and gut one,
you can eat it. Once. Some poems are
greased pigs, squirting free, leaving you
breathless, dirty, hands on your knees,
shaking your head at their dexterity.
Some are chameleons, appearing to be
whatever you want or need them to be.
I could point out a poem is miraculous
in its animal shape-shifting, not a statue
covered with a tarp to be yanked off
at a key moment. I could say it means
no more than a tree does or a sparrow
or a brick, but although this may shift
their attention from what the poem means
to what I mean, it's the kind of response
that makes people say they hate poetry.
"You want to know what the poem means?"
I ask. They nod. "I understand that,"
I say as I close my book and turn away

to wipe the board clean. Most grumble,
annoyed at this refusal to do my job,
some suspect it is another teacher trick,
a few are afraid I'm just being mean,
and one girl stares as if I'm an animal
who is moving just outside of her reach.

Strange

At mid-term, I still don't know
what Mark's voice sounds like,
so when he raises his hand
I immediately stop talking. I want
to encourage any contribution
especially since after the first week
people stopped sitting near him.
What he will say doesn't matter;
the hand itself validates my decision
to place the work of an obscure poet
on the syllabus. If even Mark has
responded to the poem, others
will have as well. I call on him.
He pauses, then slowly intones,
"Do you know that you have
a hair growing out of your eyebrow
that is this big?" He makes a gap
with his thumb and index finger.
No one laughs. They watch me,
holding themselves motionless,
the same way we did years ago
after Kevin O'Brien fell asleep
in class and Sister Ann grabbed
his long hair, pulled his head up,
then banged it down on the desk
hard enough to crack the wood.
But, it's not the nuns I find myself
remembering, instead, it's a professor
I had at Mark's age, who kept trying
to get us to say something about
red wheelbarrows, plums, jars,
a balding guy walking a beach,
poems so idiotic and bewildering
I spent most of the time considering

the enormous tufts growing wild
from his ears. They were thickets,
thistles, brambles of antennae
sweeping for signals as he insisted
every poem says the same thing:
"Look closely. This world and all
the people in it are more familiar
and more strange than you think."

Soporific

Don't worry.
This poem isn't difficult.
There are no hidden meanings
that make you feel stupid
when someone points them out.
It capitalizes the letters you expect,
it doesn't use punctuation in weird ways,
and it doesn't jam words together
or scatter them around the page.
The line breaks aren't significant;
they're only here to reassure you
this really is a poem
(and not one of those paragraphs
some people insist are poems
but you can't figure out why).
Most importantly, this poem isn't long.
It's not even a page.
It will be over soon. Like a shot or a pill.
It's not one of those unbearable poems
that go on and on sometimes
for as many as three or four pages
until you have to scan ahead to see
when it will finally be over.
No, this one is short.
In fact, you were done a little bit ago,
and this part here is just hand-holding
to make sure you don't
suffer from any ill effects.

When The Poems Came for Dinner

They arrived on time, fully dressed, and clean,
which was reassuring. They even brought
wine, covered their mouths when they sneezed,
and talked about school districts and the weather.
We began to think, "We should have The Poems
over more often," and we felt guilty at how cool
we had been towards them, but then they started
drinking. By the main course they were spilling
words everywhere and slathering around curses
like condiments. They derailed each attempt
at conversation with non-sequiturs and ignored
our stiff expressions and rigid body language
as if to say, "Hey, we're The Poems. Everyone
can fuck off. We get to say whatever we want."
At last we tricked them into leaving by pretending
the alcohol was gone, but by then they had broken
several pieces of grammar and provoked even
the mildest of us to demand, "What do you mean
by that? As we smiled apologetically at the guests
who remained, we could still hear The Poems
outside, stomp-dancing up and down the drive,
swinging mixed metaphors against the fence,
and howling *Ollie Ollie In Come Fucking Free.*

Field Trip to the Poetry Discovery Center

We walk past the cages that hold
sestinas, villanelles, and pantoums,
stopping when someone mentions
an odd coloring or unusual feature.

A few people ooh and aaah,
but it feels forced, obligatory,
since most of the poems huddle
in corners, covered with cedar shavings.

It's impossible to get a sense
of what they really look like,
how big they are, or how they move.
The plaques offer some facts and maps,

but no one looks at these very closely.
A few kids knock on the windows.
Most find a place to sit and text,
or they disappear somewhere.

A docent, who has been waiting
to answer questions, finally says,
You should see them in the wild.
There aren't many left anymore,

but when you come across one,
and it suddenly takes off . . .
He looks through a pane and sighs.
They're not like this. They're amazing.

Sestina

She says the word "sestina" makes her think
of angels, and her voice has a wistfulness
as if she's envious people used to believe
in something so beautiful. To her, sestinas
are like cathedrals, monuments built long ago,
and now visited mainly by tourists and old ladies.
We marvel at the effort, the hard work
of placing stone on stone, but can't imagine
spending much time there in the cold shadows.
As for constructing one, despite the attempts
of teachers to encourage us, we sense it takes
more than craft, choosing the right end words,
or considering it a puzzle. It requires confidence
in the power of patterns to give meaning
to our lives. It takes commitment to tradition.
Most of all, it takes faith. "Angels," she says,
and we avoid looking around at one another
as we wait for these awkward longings to pass.

Broken (Part II)

Even as successful as he is now,
Jake says he can't help thinking of her
no matter what he writes. He keeps
imagining she's approaching from behind,
a dark fluttering of wings, a piercing
Awk! and Frag! then the inexorable pinch
of talons as she tries to rip off a dangling
modifier or pry apart a noun and verb
that don't agree. Back in the bleach-scented
classrooms, I had thought of her more
like an employee of a morgue, dispassionately
identifying and marking diseased parts,
cutting them out with a clinical efficiency,
then eating lunch as we carted the corpses
away to bury. Now, however, as I find myself
lost in my own dark wood, trying to make
the simplest of shelters, each word seems rotten,
each sentence breaks at the slightest pressure,
and I too sense her perched somewhere near,
eager to descend and start worrying apart
the little I've managed to put together.

Sort of Definitive

When she said the story
was *sort of, like, fantastic,*
the teacher asked
if it was fantastic or not.
Quit hedging, he said,
and stake a position.
He railed almost daily
against *like, sort of, very,*
really, a lot, basically,
insisting: *Things are*
or they are not,
and that's enough.
"Jesus really wept a lot"
is the Bible written
by someone with no faith
in the power of words.

She knew what he meant,
but it would be years
before she understood
why he was wrong.
The earth is not a sphere
or orb, but basically one.
Light is wave and particle.
The sun is plasma
which is neither gas,
nor solid, nor liquid.
We might want things
to be different, definite,
but the universe we live in
is a sort-of kind-of place.

Salvage

Red shoes, a hero,
a villain, the bed trick,
a run to the airport
just in time,

tear what you need
from the stories,

a way to solve
problems, to make
sense, to imagine
a life continuing on
chapter by chapter.

Maybe even one
with a happy ending.

Ode

He says compose an ode, a praise song
to something ordinary, and I decide
to first write down possible subjects:
coffee, donuts, the morning air,
the smell of onions and butter frying,
the purple hyacinths by the garage,
the jeans with the holes in the knees,
and I add to the list as I walk around
the house, the neighborhood, the day,
until I've filled my notebook, so I buy
another and the first thing I write
in it is new notebooks and old cashiers
who call you honey and I fill that one
then another and the sun descends,
and I put that in—that takes dozens
of pages as the light seems to change
everything and the sun itself changes
as it dissolves against the horizon—
then the gloaming and the thickening
darkness, then the glowing of houses
blue windows bike lights fireflies
stars and smelling somebody's pipe
and woodsmoke and hearing voices
and cheers from the nearby ball field
and someone's guitar and drinking wine
that was given to you by a friend
and sitting on a screened porch swinging
a pen back and forth noting as much
as you can and trying to get some of it
down just some of it before it's too late.

According to My Friend the Astrologer

He reads my chart every year on my birthday,
and the news is never good. My planets never
align fortuitously, and some days, even months,
are bloody, but this time, he grins as he considers
the arcs and diameters. He reaches for the pot
of tea we always drink, and, after a few sips,
he says, "It's interesting because according to this,
you're dead." After a moment, I suggest,
"Should be dead? Dying?" He shakes his head.
"No, definitely dead. That's what the stars say."

After we finish the tea, he says, "I wouldn't worry
about it. I've been dead for years." I suppose
he means this to be reassuring. We burn the paper
then walk to the marina bar, and when the waitress
asks if we want to wait for a table with a view,
or take the first available, I shrug, "It doesn't matter.
Apparently everything from now on is a bonus."
My friend laughs and nods, "That's exactly
what the universe has been trying to tell you."

Sending Christmas Cards to Huck and Hamlet

They never write back,
even though at one point
we spent so much time together
I knew exactly
what they would say next.

It's disappointing,
but I understand
how each day
fills with obligations,
family responsibilities, work duties,
crises with pirates or con men
or the PTA,
so even though we keep thinking
we'll get a free moment
we never seem to.
The car needs an oil change.
The dishes need to be washed.

I imagine them,
as I do all my friends,
being the same age
as when we met,
but time's a river.
Like me, Huck must be
at least middle-aged now.
Probably each December,
he floats through a mall
or sits in a food court,
guarding his wife's bags.
As for Hamlet,
maybe he tried
a couple of graduate programs,
but he was never

much of a finisher,
so there would have been
the inevitable drift,
each girl waiting for him
to get his act together,
each job a temporary
waste of his talents.

The silence doesn't matter;
I've come to realize
letters are more
for the sender
than the receiver.
The thousands who write
Juliet know, that even dead,
she wouldn't have time
to respond to everyone.

Mail is nothing,
but a gesture
of longing,
like the stack of books
on the night stand.

I write the names,
carry them
in my hands,
then abandon them
in boxes
in moments of faith,
each envelope
a prayer
threading away
from me
binding and raveling.

Like Scout in *To Kill a Mockingbird*, **JOSEPH MILLS** doesn't remember learning to read. It's an ability he always seems to have had. As a child, he hauled around a Falstaff beer case full of comic books on his family's frequent travels. Now, he carries a bag of books on every trip. These usually go unopened because he ends up reading (and buying) what he finds on his journeys. He knows traveling would be easier without the bag, but he can't bring himself to leave it behind. He currently lives in Winston-Salem, where, to make his problem less obvious, he has divided his library among several locations, including his house, car, office and classroom at the UNC School of the Arts. This scattered collection includes his three previous poetry volumes: *Somewhere During the Spin Cycle*; *Angels, Thieves, and Winemakers*; and *Love and Other Collisions*.

Cover artist **ALIREZA DARVISH** was born in Rasht, Iran and studied History of Art and Painting at the Fine Arts Institute in Teheran, Iran. He has worked as an illustrator for many art and literature magazines, and has taught painting and drawing. His art has been featured in solo exhibitions and his animated films have been shown and have earned awards throughout Australia, Brazil, the Czech Republic, Egypt, France, Germany, Iran, Italy, South Africa, Spain, and the United States.

At the age of fifteen in Iran, Alireza says he was forced to avoid trouble by throwing into a river many books from his personal library that were prohibited by the Iranian government. Now living as a political refugee in Germany, Alireza creates art through illustrations and animations, many using books as a metaphor for the human being and his or her relationship to the world through books.

Discover more of Alireza's fascinating world of art at www.animacali.com/html/seit1.html.

CPSIA information can be obtained at www.ICGtesting.com
Printed in the USA
BVOW02s0143110216

436295BV00001B/7/P